Pass & Understand the Level 1 Award in Health and Safety in a Construction Environment.

Training & Revision

Andrew Wells.
2014

Table of Contents

Pass & Understand the Level 1 Award in Health and Safety in a Construction Environment.

The Level 1 Award in Health & Safety in a Construction Environment was created to ensure all workers on a construction site have a basic awareness of Health and Safety.

This study aid has been written to give those wishing to achieve the Award the required knowledge and background information to understand the principles of Health & Safety in a Construction Environment.

In this study aid the Award has been split into five Sections representing the five Learning Outcomes.

As you work through the book you will notice some paragraphs are *in bold and italics* and have referencing in the margin, these numbers relate to the Learning Outcomes and the Assessment Criteria to which the *paragraph* relates.

At the back of the book are the questions, these have also been referenced to the Learning Outcomes and Assessment Criteria in the Award.

When working through the answers, if you are unsure of an answer, you can simply look up the answer using the reference numbers.

Section 1
The Principles of Risk Assessment for Maintaining and Improving Health and Safety at Work.

Risk Assessments & Method Statements

1.1.1 The purpose of a Risk Assessment is to assess a hazard and decide whether you have enough precautions in place or whether you should do more.

There are many hazards in a construction environment.
To help reduce the risk of injuries to workers a Risk Assessment is carried out.
When a hazard is identified the risk is assessed and a decision is made on the level of risk and whether additional precautions should be put in place.

1.1.2 The purpose of a Method Statement is a give the worker a logical sequence of how a job is to be carried out in a safe manner and without risks to health.

Method Statements are created to give a worker a logical sequence of how a job is to be carried out in a safe manner without risks to health. The Method Statement includes all the risks identified in the risk assessment and the measures needed to control those risks.

The Legal Requirements of Risk Assessments & Method Statements

1.2.1 Employers (and self employed workers) are legally required to carry out risk assessments.

All employers and self employed workers have a legal responsibility to carry out risk assessments before they start work to ensure work is carried out in a safe manner.

1.2.2 Employees are legally required to comply with Method Statements

All employees are legally required to comply with Method Statements to ensure the work is carried out safely.

The Common Causes of Work-Related Fatalities & Injuries

1.3.1 Most fatal work-related fatalities are the result of Falls from Height

1.3.2 Most work-related injuries are caused by Slips and Trips.

Several thousand construction workers are injured each year following a trip or slip whilst at work on a building site. Around 1000 of these injuries involve someone fracturing bones or dislocating joints.

Most could be avoided by the effective management of working areas and access routes, such as stairwells, corridors and footpaths.

Below and on the following pages is a list and description of actual accidents that have occurred, resulting in the deaths of workers;

1   Falls from Ladders
2   Falls through Fragile Roofs
3   Lifting Operations
4   Struck by Plant
5   Overturning Plant

6   Falls from Scaffolds
7   Falls down Internal Voids
8   Asphyxiation by Fumes
9   Accidents in excavations
10   Trapped and crushed while operating a MEWP

Falls from Ladders

The foreman arrives on site. He is in a hurry and decides to do a quick repair.

The foreman stepped onto the ladder on the roof and the ladder slid down.

Falls through Fragile Roofs

One of the windows had been hidden from view.

One of the roofers falls through the sheets to the floor below sustaining fatal head injuries.

Lifting Operations

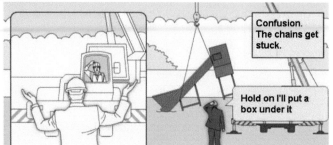

Not knowing the correct hand signals to communicate to the driver, the driver had difficulty understanding what he wanted.
A corner of the conveyor became stuck, the driver lowers it and the chains become slack.

A steel box is placed under one end of the conveyor as a temporary support. Second man crawls under the conveyor to try to release the corner crowbar.

The second man tries to move the conveyor away from the obstructions, it moves suddenly, slips off the box crushing the man.

Struck by Plant

The site labourer positions himself behind the lorry and in front of a generator that was providing power to a noisy jack-hammer.

Overturning Plant

Although the driver had been taught the correct way to go up and down slopes he panicked when faced with a steeper slope than he had experienced before.

The dumper tipped and because the driver's seat-belt was loose he was ejected forward and the truck fell on top of him.

Falls from Scaffold

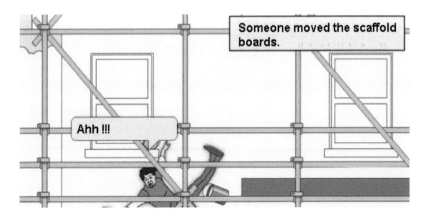

The boards are moved and there is still some painting and decorating to be finished. A painter arrives to touch up the windows after the bricklayers have left.

Falls down Internal Voids

The labourer was trying to maneuver the heavy breaker in to position when he over balanced and fell 7 metres down the lift shaft, sustaining in fatal injuries.

The void should have been protected.

Asphyxiation by Fumes

A diesel powered water pump was hired to clear a flood in the basement that a company had built. The hire company had not provided any specific warning as to the risks of carbon monoxide poisoning.

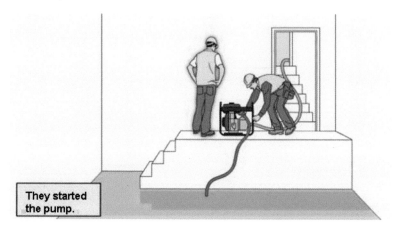

The two men installed the pump in a dry area inside the basement and set it running.

After a couple of hours one of the workers returned to the basement. Because the room wasn't ventilated and the door was closed, the worker was slowly overcome with fumes and died.

Accidents in excavations

A man is in the deepest part of the trench when the dumper drew up to the edge.

The inside of the trench collapsed, completely covering the worker. The weight of the soil made it impossible to dig the worker out before he was asphyxiated.

Trapped and crushed while operating a Mobile Elevated Working Platform (MEWP)

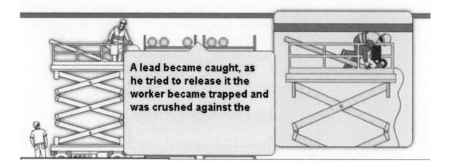

A lead became caught, as he tried to release it the worker became trapped and was crushed against the

The lead from one of the workers tools nearly got caught on the warehouse racking. The worker had to learn out of the MEWP basket to keep the lead from getting snagged, he then got trapped and crushed between the roof and the MEWP .

The implications of not preventing accidents and ill health at work.

1.4   Accidents and ill health can ruin lives and affect businesses.

If someone at work gets killed it has a devastating effect on all those around him
If someone gets injured or is off work due to ill health, it also has financial implications

Accidents and ill health can affect businesses, If output is lost,   or machinery is damaged the work program will be affected, this could incur costs due to the delays.

If someone is killed or injured, insurance costs will increase, the employer may have to go to court and could be charged with negligence.

The definitions of accident, near miss, hazard, risk and competence.

1.5.1 Accident:- *"any unplanned event that results in personnel injury or damage to property, plant or equipment".*

1.5.2 Near-miss:- *"an unplanned event which does not cause injury or damage, but could have done so."*

Examples include: tools or debris falling from height close to workers and incidents involving vehicles and electrical short-circuits.

1.5.3 Hazard:- *A hazard is something that can cause adverse effects.*

For example:
Water on a staircase is a hazard, because you could slip on it, fall and hurt yourself.
Loud noise is a hazard because it can cause hearing loss.
Inhaling asbestos dust is a hazard because it can cause cancer.

1.5.4 Risk:- *A risk is the likelihood that a hazard will actually cause an accident and the likelihood of it happening.*

Risk is a two-part concept and you have to have both parts to make sense of it.

Likelihoods can be expressed as probabilities (e.g. "one in a thousand"), frequencies (e.g. "1000 cases per year") or in a qualitative way (e.g. "negligible", "significant", etc.).

The effect can be described in many different ways. For example:

The annual risk of a worker in Great Britain experiencing a fatal accident [effect] at work [hazard] is less than one in 100,000 [likelihood];

About 1500 workers each year [likelihood] in Great Britain suffer a non-fatal major injury [effect] from contact with moving machinery [hazard]; or

The lifetime risk of an employee developing asthma [effect] from exposure to substance X [hazard] is significant [likelihood].

1.5.5 Competence:- *"Having the knowledge and ability to carry out the work and be aware of the risks involved".*

To be competent an organisation or individual must have sufficient knowledge of the tasks to be undertaken and the risks involved and the experience and ability to carry out their duties in relation to the project, to recognise their limitations and take appropriate action to prevent harm to those carrying out construction work, or those affected by the work

Typical hazards/risks

1.6.1 There are a wide range of typical hazards that can be associated with the resources or materials you may use, these can include;

Substances that are hazardous to health, these will have a COSHH warning and must be handled safely

Sharp edges can cause cuts and require you to wear gloves to protect your hands.

Heavy or awkward to lift resources, unless you lift them correctly you could injure your back.

Poorly stacked resources can fall causing injury.

1.6.2 Typical hazards with equipment you may use include;

Incorrectly fitted or missing safety guards (putting the user at risk of serious accidents).

Faulty wiring or plugs on electrical equipment is a *hazard (putting the user at risk of electrocution).*

Vibrating tools can cause 'Vibration hand-arm syndrome (HAVS), an industrial injury triggered by continuous use of vibrating hand-held machinery. HAVS is a disorder that affects the blood vessels, nerves, muscles, and joints, of the hand, wrist, and arm.

Lack of training in the use of equipment can lead to accidents through misuse or lack of appropriate safety equipment

1.6.3 Typical hazards associated with obstructions include;
Trip Hazards, many accidents are caused simply because there is something in the way causing a ***trip hazard***, such as building materials or waste.
Blocked Emergency Escape Routes are an obvious hazard in the case of an emergency evacuation.

1.6.4 Typical Hazards Associated with Storage include;

Flammable materials which are a fire risk.
Badly stacked resources can fall, causing injures.
Leaking chemicals can release toxic fumes and *environmental contamination.*
Trip Hazards, Storage areas must be kept tidy and pedestrian routes clear to prevent trip hazards.

1.6.5 Hazards Associated with Services.

Buried Gas and Electrical Services can cause fires and electrocution.
Overhead power lines are a hazard with the risk of electrocution.
Underground cables pose a risk of electrocution.

Overhead Power Lines
Any work near electric overhead power lines must be carefully planned and carried out to avoid danger from accidental contact or close proximity to the lines.

Buried Services

Buried services pose a particular hazard.

Work needs to be carefully planed and the Method Statement followed.

Precautions the use of plans, cable locating devices and safe digging practices.

The most accurate way to locate buried services is with the use of Trial Holes.

If you need to dig near the underground services you should <u>not</u> use a jack hammer, a pick and fork or an excavator.

You should use a spade or shovel.

If, when digging you find a run of yellow plastic marker tape this means there is a buried service and further excavation must be carried out with care. If you hit and damage a buried cable, you should not touch the cable, you must stop work and report it immediately.

If you are in a deep trench and start to feel dizzy you should make sure that you and any others get out quickly as there could be noxious or toxic gasses present.

Refurbishment work presents the greatest risk of electrocution and must be planned, managed and monitored to ensure that workers are not exposed to risk from electric shock.

1.6.6 Hazards Associated with Waste. There are a range of hazards associated with the different kinds of waste.

Trip Hazards, an untidy site where waste has not been disposed of creates trip hazards.

Fire Risks, wood, packaging, and paint left lying around create fire risks

Food waste must be disposed of carefully so as not to encourage rats which might be carrying *Weils Disease.*

Health Hazards, *asbestos waste* is a health hazard and should only be removed by approved contractors.

Environmental Contamination, hazardous waste such as empty paint cans, fluorescent tubes or gypsum based products based must be disposed of in the appropriate container to prevent *environmental contamination.*

1.6.7 Hazards Associated with Work Activities

There are many hazards associated with work activities these include;
Working at Height

Poorly maintained tools.

Trip hazards.

Nails left sticking out of wood.

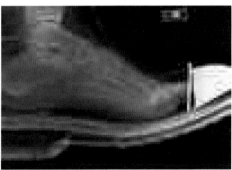

The photo is an X-ray image of a nail which has gone through the sole of a workers boot into the worker's foot.

Unauthorised people should be kept out of the work areas due to the hazards associated with of work activities and the risk of injury to other workers or members of the public through work activities.

The importance of reporting accidents and near misses.

Reporting accidents and near misses allows us to learn from them and everyone will benefit from working in a safer work environment.

Near misses are a warning that an accident could have taken place and enables us to learn lessons and put a safe method of work in place before a serious incident occurs , maybe involving you or a working colleague.

Reporting near-misses also helps management to identify trends and faults within the system and introduce effective control measures.

A report tells the enforcing authorities for occupational health and safety (HSE and local authorities) about serious incidents and cases of disease.
This means they can identify where and how risks arise and whether they need to be investigated.

It also allows HSE and local authorities to target their work and provide advice on how to avoid work-related deaths, injuries, ill health and accidental loss.

1.7   Reporting and recording accidents are legal requirements.

Reporting accidents and near misses identifies hazards where a risk assessment could help develop a Method Statement and reduce the potential risks.

Typical accident reporting procedures

The accident reporting procedure should be explained during Induction.

Typically the Accident Reporting Procedure would be;

1.8   If someone is injured they should report it to the site manager as soon as possible and enter it into the accident book.

If the injured person is unable to enter it then someone else who was present at the time should enter the details of the accident.

If it is a serious accident the Site Manager must inform the Health & Safety Executive (HSE).

In more detail;

1. All accidents must be entered in the appropriate Accident Book either by the injured person or, if this is not practical, someone else present at the time.

2. An accident Report form (Part 1 only) is to be completed by the same person who should then give the form to the immediate supervisor of the injured person.

3 The Immediate Superior must then:-
   Note that the accident has occurred.
   Ensure that the Accident Book has been correctly and fully completed.
   Immediately pass the Accident Report form to the Safety Manager.
   Enter on clockcard, or other such notification to the Wages Department, the words "Injured at Work".

4.   The Safety Manager will then:-
     Ensure that, where applicable, the requirements of the Reporting of Injuries, Diseases and Dangerous Occurrences Regulations 1995 are met.
     Complete Part II of the Company Accident Report form, recording the findings of the subsequent investigation.
     Discuss the accident and the contributory factors with the Departmental head
     Report findings to the Director responsible for Health & Safety and, if necessary, instigate any disciplinary proceedings.
     Ensure the Accounts Department have been informed that the accident occurred to enable their procedures to be implemented.

5.   The Director responsible for Health & Safety will then:-
     Ensure, so far as reasonably practical, that proper action is taken to help prevent the accident being repeated.

Who is responsible for making accident reports.

1.9   *The injured person or, if this is not practical, someone else present at the time complete part 1 of the Accident Book.*

Their immediate supervisor must immediately pass the Accident Report form to the Safety Manager.

The Safety Manager will then notify the HSE if appropriate (ensuring the requirements of the Reporting of Injuries, Diseases and Dangerous Occurrences Regulations 1995 are met).

Section 2 The Importance of Safe Manual Handling.

Manual handling is the biggest cause of injury in the construction environment.

Manual handling includes lifting, lowering, pushing, pulling and carrying;

Handling heavy objects is not the only cause of injury.

Harm can also result from doing a task repetitively, even if the load is relatively light (e.g. bricklaying), or where the person's body position is less than ideal (e.g. tying rebar).

The reasons for ensuring safe manual handling in the workplace.

Manual handling relates to the moving of items either by lifting, lowering, carrying, pushing or pulling.

Injuries can be caused not just by the weight but also the amount of times you have to pick up or carry an item, the distance you are carrying it, the height you are picking it up from or putting it down. and any twisting, bending stretching or other awkward posture you may get in whilst doing a task.

An injured person may find that their ability to do their job is affected and this will have an impact on their lifestyle, leisure activities, ability to sleep and future job prospects.

It is essential that employers manage the risks to their employees.

If possible you should not carry out any manual handling tasks and, where they are necessary, you should reduce the risk by using lifting equipment - trolleys, fork lifts etc.

Where tasks are essential and cannot be done using lifting equipment, conveyors or wheeled trolleys/cages, a suitable and sufficient risk assessment should be conducted.

2.1   *Unsafe Manual Handling causes accidents which could lead to permanent disabilities.*

In addition; Employers may have to bear substantial costs, through lost production, sickness absence costs of retraining, wages/overtime to cover for the absent person and potentially compensation payments.

The potential injuries and ill health that may occur from incorrect manual handling.

2.2   *Your back is the most likely part of your body to be injured due to incorrect manual handling.*

Injuries caused by incorrect manual handling include;
Sciatica (a very painful and debilitating condition where the sciatic nerve is trapped).
Slipped Discs (a common back condition caused through incorrect manual handling) and
Musculoskeletal Disorders (MSDs) such as ***upper and lower limb pain/disorders, joint and repetitive strain injuries.***.

Your responsibilities when Moving and Storing materials, Manual Handling and Using Mechanical Lifting.

2.3   *You have a legal responsibility to comply with your employer's Method Statement when moving or storing materials, when manual handling or when using mechanical lifting equipment.*

You must not use any mechanical lifting aids unless you have been trained in their use.

The procedures for safe lifting in accordance with official guidance.

Before you attempt to lift a heavy or awkward load you should plan how to lift it safely.

You need to consider its size and condition, whether it has handholds and the weight.
The safest way to find out if the load is too heavy to lift is to find out the weight of the load, there is often a warning put on a label.

Before attempting to lift a large load you should always try dividing it into smaller loads.
Alternatively get someone to help you or use a mechanical lifting aid.

If you need to lift the load which is not heavy but is so big you can't see in front of you, you should ask for help to carry the load so that you can both see ahead. If someone is going to help you it is important that both of you are about the same size and can lift the same weight.

2.4 *If you have to lift a load, follow your employers Method Statement. Use Kinetic Lifting Techniques.*

Kinetic Lifting
If you need to lift a load from the floor you should stand with your feet slightly apart and your knees bent, you should keep your back straight and use the strength of your leg muscles to lift.

| | | | |
| A | B | C | D |

A   **Estimate weight, ensure path is clear.**
B   Knees bent, Back straight, Feet slightly apart, Elbows in, Firm grip.
C   Maintain correct posture, lift smoothly.
D   Maintain correct posture whilst lowering.

If you need to move a load, which is heavier on one side than the other you should pick it up on the heavy side towards you.
If you have to twist or turn your body when you lift or place a load, it means the weight you can lift safely is less than usual.

If you have to move a load while you're sitting, not standing, you can lift less than usual.
Also if you need to reach above your head and lower the load to the floor, it will be more difficult to keep your back straight and your chin in, you will therefore put extra stress on your arms and your back, plus the load will be more difficult to control.

If you have to carry a load down a steep slope you should first assess whether you can still carry the load safely.

If you have been told how to handle a heavy load and you think there's a better way to do it, you should discuss it with your supervisor.

The importance of using site safety equipment when handling materials and equipment.

Site safety equipment is provided for your safety, you should use it as instructed.
Never interfere with site safety equipment.

2.5   *You must use site safety equipment that is provided for your safety to protect you from injuries.*

Lifting Aids to assist manual handling in the workplace.

There are a range of aides that may be available to assist you in manual handling, these include;

2.6 Brick Grabbers, Sack Barrows, Trolley Forks, Wheel Barrows, Jenny Wheels, and the Genie Lift.

Brick Grabbers	Sack barrow	Trolley forks
Wheel Barrow	Jenny wheel	Genie Lift

How to apply safe work practices, follow procedures and report problems when carrying out safe manual handling in the workplace.

2.7 *Use mechanical lifting equipment if it is available.*
If lifting by hand use kinetic lifting procedures
Comply with the Risk Assessment and Method Statement.

Report any problems to your supervisor immediately.

Section 3 The Importance of Working Safely at Height.

Falls from height are the most common kind of accident causing fatal injuries in construction.

In 2010/11, 26 per cent of all fatal construction accidents were the result of a fall from height.

All these accidents would have been preventable, and everything possible needs to be done to ensure that this type of accident does not continue occurring.

The Definition of Working at Height

3.1   Working at Height is "working at any height where a person could be injured falling from it".

There is no minimum height that could be considered as working at height.

Your responsibilities when Working at Height

It is your responsibility when working at height to use all the equipment which has been provided for you in the correct and proper manner and to follow all   training and instruction.

You must report any hazards or faulty or dangerous equipment to your supervisor

You must not interfere or alter any access or safety equipment unless qualified.

3.2   Use access and safety equipment as instructed and never interfere with access or safety equipment,
Report all hazards or dangerous equipment immediately and follow the Method Statement

Hazards/risks associated with working at height

In 2010/11, 26 per cent of all fatal construction accidents were the result of a fall from height.

All these accidents would have been preventable, and everything possible needs to be done to ensure that this type of accident does not continue occurring.

There are a wide rang of risks associated with working at height, these include; Dropping tools and debris, instability of ladders, overhead cables, fragile roofs, scaffolds, internal voids, equipment, the working area and other people.

3.3.1 Dropping tools and debris from a height can cause death or injury to those below.

The hazard can be prevented by erecting barriers to keep people away from the danger zone and by using guards and netting to prevent tools and debris from falling.

Instability of Ladders

3.3.2 Ladders can slip sideways and outwards

Sideways slipping at upper resting   point can be caused by due to over-reaching or instability.

Outwards slipping at the bottom of the ladder can be due to unsuitable ground conditions or the ladder being at an incorrect angle.

These hazards can be minimized by;

Using on hard, flat, level surface.
Stabilise the ladder by tying to a suitable point to prevent movement, (or use proprietary stability devices).
Ensure ladders are fitted with anti-slip feet

Place ladders at correct angle (75 degrees or 1m out for every 4 m up).
Rest the top against a suitable firm surface (not plastic gutters, glass or infill panels).
Ensure ladder rungs and stiles are clean and not slippery
Ladder accessories may improve stability and should be used where appropriate, e.g. stile extensions for stability on slopes.

Overhead Cables

3.3.3 Overhead cables present a hazard of electric shock, which can cause death by electrocution or a loss of balance resulting in a fall from height.

Fragile Roofs

3.3.4 Falls through fragile roofs and fragile roof lights cause death and serious injury.

Falls through fragile roofs account for almost a fifth of all the fatal accidents which result from a fall from height in the construction industry. On average 7 people are killed each year after falling through a fragile roof or fragile roof light. Many others suffer permanent disabling injury.

Tube Scaffolds

3.3.5 Hazards associated with Tube Scaffolds include missing boards and guard rails.

Hazards are created when boards are moved or guards are interfered with, this resulting in an increased *risk* of falls from the scaffold or tools or debris falling on people under the scaffold.

Scaffolds should only be erected and altered by a qualified scaffolder and should never be altered or interfered with by an unqualified worker.

Moving or un-securing a ladder can make a ladder unstable resulting in falls from the ladder.

Mobile Scaffolds

3.3.6 Hazards associated with Mobile Scaffolds include; scaffolds incorrectly erected, missing or incorrect guard rails, and accessing the platform by climbing up the outside.

Many people are injured each year when they fall from towers or when the tower overturns.

Towers should only be erected by trained and competent people.

The incidents that occur are mainly caused by:

The Method Statement is not adhered to when erecting or dismantling a *tower scaffold*,

Missing *guard-rails*

A *ladder being* leant against the tower scaffold can cause the *tower scaffold to overturn*.

Riding on a mobile scaffold whilst it is being moved.

Internal Voids

3.3.7 Internal voids such as lift shafts and holes in the floor (for services) create a serious hazard with the risk of workers falling through the voids to the floors below.

The labourer was trying to maneuver the heavy breaker in to position when he over balanced and fell 7 metres down the lift shaft, sustaining in fatal injuries.

The void should have been protected.

Equipment

3.3.8 The Hazards associated with Equipment include poor maintenance and not following the instructions for use.

Maintenance
Poorly maintained access equipment can *hazardous* due to a range of defects with the *risk* of the equipment *collapsing* while in use causing injury to the use
If the equipment has brakes fitted they should be in working order to prevent the **risk** of the equipment moving whilst in use.
Old cracked scaffold boards will create a *hazard* as there is a *risk* the boards will snap.

Erecting
The manufacturer's instructions must be read and adhered to, in order to reduce the *risk* of accidents when erecting or dismantling access equipment
Access equipment erected on an even surface is a *hazard* as there is a *risk* the it might *topple over* injuring the user.
Access equipment erected on a soft surface can be a *hazard* as there is a *risk* the it sink into the surface becoming unstable.

Use
Overloaded access equipment creates a *hazard*, the equipment may collapse with the *risk* of injury to people working nearby
Access equipment used without a guard-rail is a *hazard*, as there is a *risk* of falling off
Over-reaching creates a hazard as there is a *risk* of the equipment toppling over.

Hop-Ups

An uneven base is a hazard when using a hop up.
There is a risk the hop-up might topple over causing the user to fall.

If the user is distracted there is a risk the user may step off the hop-up, causing injury.

Podium Steps

Podium steps are very safe to use, however faulty brakes would be a hazard.
If the brakes did not work there would be a risk of the podium rolling downhill.

When working at a high level the podium would need stabilisers to reduce the risk of the podium toppling over.

The manufacturer's instructions must be read and adhered to when erecting or dismantling the podium.

Step Ladders

There are a range of hazards associated with step-ladders.
Poorly maintained step-ladders can fail.

Steps used on a soft surface could sink into the surface..

Steps used on an uneven surface can rock causing the user to *loose balance* and fall .

Over-reaching on steps is hazardous as there is a risk of the steps toppling over.

Trestle Scaffolding

Trestle scaffolding can be very dangerous to work on due to several hazards.

Trestle scaffolds set up on an uneven or soft surface are hazardous with a risk of collapse.

Having no guard-rail is a hazard, as there is a *risk* of falling off.

Over spaced trestles are another hazard, there is the risk of the unsupported boards snapping, or the trestles becoming unstable.

Old cracked scaffold boards will create a hazard as there is a *risk* the boards will give way.

Overloaded trestles are a hazard. The scaffold can collapse with the *risk* of injury to people working on or near the trestles.

The Work Area

3.3.9 Hazards associated with The Work Area include; trip hazards, missing guardrails, open access gates, and unprotected voids.

Trip hazards can caused by trailing leads, tools poorly stacked materials and debris.

Materials stacked higher than brick guards to present a risk of materials falling onto people below.

Open access gates give rise to a risk of falls from height.

Other People

3.3.10 The Hazards associated with Other People include; people working above dropping objects onto people below.

People working above you put you at risk from tools or debris dropping from height.

People working below you are at risk of Injury from falling tools etc.

How hazards/risks associated with working at height can be controlled.

3.4   The Hazards and Risks associated with working at height can be controlled by complying with Risk Assessments and Method Statements.

Inspect access equipment before use and report any hazards or problems you identify.

Never put yourself in danger.

The regulation that controls the use of suitable equipment for working at height.

3.5   *The Work at Height Regulations* *controls the use of suitable equipment for working at height.*

The Work at Height Regulations exist to prevent death and injury caused by a fall from height.

If you are an employer or you control work at height (for example facilities managers or building owners who may contract others to work at height) the Regulations apply to you.

Employers
Employers and those in control of any work at height activity must make sure work is properly planned, supervised and carried out by competent people. This includes using the right type of equipment for working at height.

Employees
Employees have legal obligations to take reasonable care of themselves and others who may be affected by their actions, and to cooperate with their employer to enable their health and safety policies and requirements to be complied with.

Section 4   The Risks to Health Within a Construction Environment.

Substances Hazardous to health

4.1   Substances that are commonly found on site and that are Hazardous to Health include;
Acids (burns), Adhesives (fumes), Alkali (burns). Asbestos (lung diseases), Cement (burns), Concrete (burns), Diesel (skin diseases, environmental), Gases (toxic, explosive), Hydraulic Fluid (skin diseases, environmental), Insulating materials (lung diseases, skin irritant), Lead (poison, environmental), Mortar additives (various), Oils (skin, environmental), Paints (toxic, lung disease, environmental) ,Petrol (skin, lung, fire, environmental), Plaster (Gypsum)(skin, lung, environmental), Thinners (toxic, skin, explosive).

Substances Hazardous to Health have to carry a warning.

DANGER HAZARD /	CORROSIVE (can burn you)	IRRITANT / HARMFULL	TOXIC (can kill you)

These substances include; chemicals and products containing chemicals, fumes and dusts, vapors and mists and gases and asphyxiating gases.

Common risks to health

4.2   *Common risks to Health include; Exposure to Asbestos, Exposure to Silica, Exposure to Excessive Noise, Exposure to Excessive Vibration and Manual Handling.*

In addition;
Direct sunlight can cause **skin cancer,**
contaminated land or water can give you **tetanus**
Weils disease (leptospirosis) is spread through rat urine.

Exposure To Silica

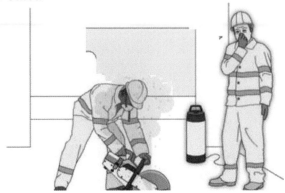

Concrete dust will contain varying amount of respirable crystalline silica or RCS. John does not know what RCS dust is or the risks to his lungs linked to breathing it in. He cuts the concrete without water suppression or a suitable mask that has been fitted to his face.

After 15 years doing similar work, john has been diagnosed with silicosis, a type of lung disease. Pain and shortness of breath prevent him from working on site or playing football with his son at the weekend. He is likely to die prematurely of heart failure bought on by his condition.

Exposure To Asbestos

Work with asbestos can release small fibres into the air. Breathing in these fibres can eventually lead to a number of fatal diseases. These include:

Asbestosis or fibrosis (scarring) of the lungs;

Lung cancer; and

Mesothelioma, a cancer of the inner lining of the chest wall or abdominal cavity.

There is no cure for asbestos-related diseases.

James worked at many sites over the following decades, growing in confidence as he completed a large range of jobs. But he never really developed an awareness of the risks of asbestos.

Thirty years after he joined the industry, James is diagnosed with a terminal cancer, mesothelioma. He is unable to work and has been told he only has a short time to live.

Manual Handling

Some blocks needed to be laid high up but a safe working platform had not been provided to help the bricklayers reach comfortably.

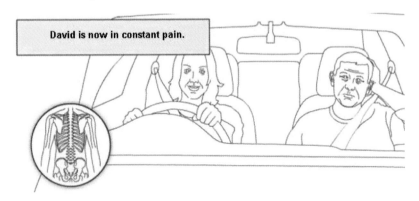

David has developed a disabling pain in his lower back, which prevents him from working on the site altogether. He is in too much pain to drive or perform simple everyday tasks in the home.

Exposure To Excessive Noise

Noise may be a problem in your work area if you have to shout to be clearly heard by someone who is standing 2 m away. If you have to work in a' hearing protection zone' you must wear hearing protection at all times. If someone near you is using noisy equipment and you have no hearing protection you should leave the area until you have the correct PPE.

Hearing Protection

If you wear hearing protection it will reduce the noise to an acceptable level. Two recommended ways to protect your hearing are the use of earplugs or ear defenders. if an ear pad is missing from an ear defender, you should not work in noisy areas until it is replaced. If you need to wear hearing protection you must remember that you may be less aware of what is going on around you. Noise can cause headaches and loss of hearing.

The damage to Steve's hearing was not immediately noticeable but now he suffers constant fining in his ears.

Steve's hearing is permanently damaged. He can't hear his friend's conversation properly and will experience poor hearing for the rest of his life.

Exposure To Excessive Vibration

Vibration is a serious health issue because it can cause a disabling injury that cannot be cured. Vibration white finger is a sign of damage to your hands and arms that might not go away, it is caused by damage to the blood vessels and nerves in your fingers and hands. Early signs of vibration white finger are; a temporary loss of feeling in the fingers, a tingling in the fingers, and the fingertips go white.

If you have any of the symptoms you should report them before they cause a problem.

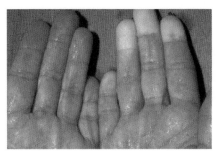

Prevention

Using a hammer drill can cause vibration white finger.

If you have to use a vibrating tool your supervisor must tell you about the risk assessment and explain the safest way to use the tool.

You can help reduce the risk of hand arm vibration by not gripping the tool to tightly. You are also less likely to suffer from hand-arm vibration if you are warm and dry.

You can reduce the effects of hand arm vibration if you do the work in short spells.

Wearing anti-vibration gloves can help prevent vibration white finger.

Jamie had been using the wall chaser since the start of the day (3 hours earlier.

Jamie had continues to regularly use vibrating tools for a number of years and had avoided health surveillance. He now has constant numbness in his hands.

The types of hazards/risks that may occur in the workplace linked with use of drugs and alcohol.

4.5 *The use of alcohol and illegal drugs make people unsafe at work. Risks include trips and falls, accidents with machinery etc.*

If your doctor has given you some medication, you should consider whether it will it make you *sleepy or unsafe to work*.

Users of illegal drugs are a *hazard* to everyone on-site as their judgment is impaired, they at *risk* of having an accident which puts everyone in danger.

Anyone who has a couple of pints of beer at lunch-time should stay off site for the rest of the day as they too become a *hazard,* putting everyone at *risk* of being injured if they have, or cause, an accident.

The importance of the correct storage of combustibles and chemicals on site.

4.4 *Incorrect storage of combustibles or chemicals could result in fires and environmental damage and pollution.*

Each year there are a number of serious fires on construction sites and buildings undergoing refurbishment.
Many could be avoided by careful planning and control of work activities.

Any outbreak of fire threatens the safety of those on site and will be

costly in damage and delay.
It can also be a hazard to people in surrounding properties.

Chemicals must be stored correctly as they can be hazardous to health and the environment if they are spilt.

The importance of personal hygiene

4.5 **Personal hygiene is important because infections such as Tetanus can be caught from contaminated soil and water. Weil's Disease (which can be fatal) is spread by rats.**

If you get a hazardous substance on your hands it can pass to your mouth when you eat (wear protective gloves while you work and wash your hands with **soap and water** *before eating*

Protect any open cut, you could get an infection called tetanus from contaminated land or water which gets into your body through an open cut in your skin.

Rats spread Weils Disease through their urine, wash your hands before eating and after work.

The potential hazards/risks to the health of workers exposed to asbestos.

Working with asbestos can release small fibres into the air.

4.6 **Inhaling asbestos fibres can lead to a number of fatal diseases.**
These diseases include:
Asbestosis or fibrosis (scarring) of the lungs,
Lung cancer,
Mesothelioma, a cancer of the inner lining of the chest wall or abdominal cavity.

There is no cure for asbestos-related diseases.

Types of asbestos waste.

Asbestos is likely to be in a building if :
it was built or refurbished between 1950 and 1980 and particularly;
if it also has a steel frame; and/or
it has boilers with thermal insulation.
Asbestos cement has also been widely used as a building material since the 1950s.

Types of asbestos waste includes;

4.7   ***Asbestos Insulating Board* (AIB)**   Used in ceilings, windows and door panels. AIB can generate high levels of fibres if cut or drilled. If in good condition, it should be left undisturbed.

Sprayed coating. Found as fire protection on structural supports (eg columns and beams). It is a high hazard asbestos product and can generate very high fibre levels if disturbed.

Textured decorative coatings. Textured coatings, like Artex, contain a small amount of asbestos.

Pipe insulation. Asbestos thermal pipe lagging is a high hazard asbestos product.

Floor tiles. Vinyl (PVC) or thermoplastic tiles contain asbestos.

Asbestos cement roof sheeting. Often found on industrial building roofs and walls.

Rainwater items. Roof gutters and downpipes were often made of asbestos cement.

Water tanks and toilet cisterns

Loose asbestos in ceiling and wall cavities

The types of personal protective equipment (PPE) used when dealing with hazardous materials

4.8   Gloves, eye protection and suitable breathing protection must be used when working with hazardous materials

Skin must be protected using suitable *gloves.*

Eye protection must be worn to protect the eyes from hazardous liquid which could splash into your eyes

Dust masks must be worn to protect the lungs from damage from dust particles.

Respiratory protective equipment (RPE) must be worn to protect you from hazardous fumes and mists

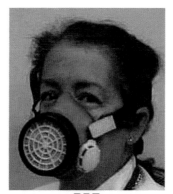

RPE

Section 5 The Importance of Working around Plant and Equipment Safely.

Serious accidents can occur when working around plant and equipment.

Ways in which moving machinery can cause injuries.

5.1 *Moving machinery can cause injuries in a variety of ways;*
You could be crushed if the driver cannot see you.
A load being lifted could be dropped.

If you **walk behind** a reversing fork lift, you may be in the operator's 'Blind Spot' and he will not be able to see you, this puts you at **risk** of being **crushed to death**.

Walking under a raised load puts you at **risk** of the load falling on top of you, causing **injury or death**.

The labourer standing behind a reversing lorry put himself at *risk* of *being crushed* between the lorry and the generator.

The hazards/risks relating to the use of plant and equipment.

5.2   *Noise, dust, electrocution, HAVS and Injuries due to incorrect or missing safety guards, incorrect use of plant & equipment and poorly maintained access equipment.*

Noise
Plant or equipment can create a noise hazard putting the user at risk of permanent damage to their hearing and even deafness.

Dust
Cutting tools can create dust, silica dust is a hazard that puts the operator and those around him at risk of silicosis (a lung disease, which can bring about premature death).

Electrocution
Hazards such as bare wires, broken switches, cracked casing and damaged plugs, are a risk of electrocution.

HAVS (Vibration White Finger)
Vibrating tools such as electric drills and pneumatic drills, put the user at risk of hand-arm vibration syndrome (HAVS)

Ineffective Safety Guards
Poorly maintained equipment can have damaged, wrongly fitted or missing safety guards, causing serious accidents.

Plant

Driving a dumper an incorrectly fastened seat belt puts the user at risk of being crushed should the dumper tip over.

Access Equipment

Damaged or overloaded scaffolding

Damaged or overloaded scaffolding can collapse, causing injuries to those using the scaffold and people nearby.

MEWPs (Mobile Elevated Working Platforms)

Using mobile elevated working platforms puts the operator at risk of hazards such as being crushed.

(An operator of a mobile elevated working platform was detracted and did not notice how close he was to the roof, he got trapped and was crushed to death)

The importance of keeping a safe distance away from plant/machinery and equipment until clear contact is made with the operator.

5.3 *If the operator does not know where you are, there is a risk of you being injured.*

It is important to keep a safe distance away from plant/machinery and equipment until you have clear contact with the operator, who will tell you when it is safe to pass.

How method statements can assist in ensuring the safety of workers where moving plant is in use.

5.3   Method Statements inform the operator how to work safely. Method Statements inform you of how to stay safe when moving plant is in use.

Method Statements will instruct workers to keep to the pedestrian walkways

Ways to eliminate or control hazards/risks relating to working around plant and equipment.

5.4   Hazards relating to working around plant and equipment can be eliminated or controlled by using pedestrian walkways and complying with site safety rules and signage.

All workers must comply with health and safety instructions and with risk assessments and method statements.

All plant and equipment operators should be qualified for the job they are doing.

Hazard warning signs and symbols used around the use of plant and equipment.

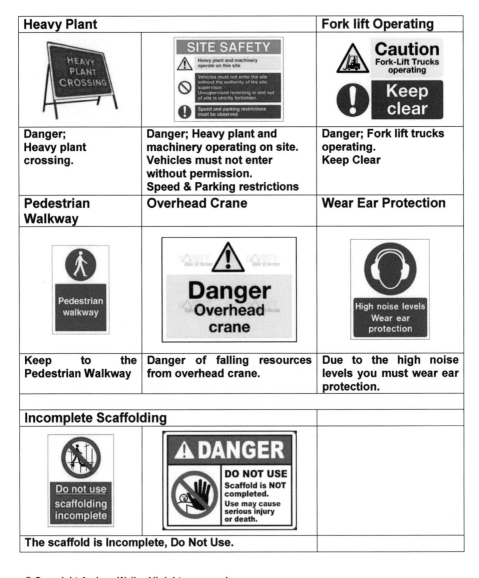

Heavy Plant		Fork lift Operating
Danger; Heavy plant crossing.	Danger; Heavy plant and machinery operating on site. Vehicles must not enter without permission. Speed & Parking restrictions	Danger; Fork lift trucks operating. Keep Clear
Pedestrian Walkway	Overhead Crane	Wear Ear Protection
Keep to the Pedestrian Walkway	Danger of falling resources from overhead crane.	Due to the high noise levels you must wear ear protection.
Incomplete Scaffolding		
The scaffold is Incomplete, Do Not Use.		

Questions

Section 1 Questions
The principles of risk assessment for maintaining and improving health and safety at work

1.1.1	**What is the purpose of a risk assessment?**
1.1.2	**What is the purpose of a method statement?**
1.2.1	**Who has a legal responsibility to make risk assessments?**
1.2.2	**What are your legal responsibilities to method statements?**
1.3.1	**What are the common causes of fatalities on a construction site?**

1.3.2	What are the common causes of injuries on a construction site?
1.4	What could happen if you did not prevent accidents and ill health at work?
1.5.1	What does the word *'accident'* mean?
1.5.2	What is a *'near-miss'*?
1.5.3	What is a hazard?
1.5.4	What does 'risk' mean?

1.5.5	What is 'competence'?
1.6.1	Describe a typical hazard with the materials you use.
1.6.2	Describe a typical hazard with the equipment you use.
1.6.3	Describe a typical hazard with obstructions at work.
1.6.4	Describe a typical hazard with the storage of materials or tools you use.
1.6.5	What are the typical hazards/risks associated with 'services' such as buried gas or electrical services.

1.6.6	Describe a typical hazard or risk associated with 'waste'.
1.6.7	Describe a typical hazards/risks associated with 'work on a construction site'.
1.7	Why is it important to report accidents and near misses
1.8	How is an accident reported on a construction site?
1.9	Who is responsible for reporting accidents?

Section 2 Questions
The importance of safe manual handling in the workplace.

2.1	What are the reasons for ensuring safe manual handling in the workplace?
2.2	How could you injure yourself through incorrect manual handling?
2.3	What are your responsibilities when moving and storing materials, manual handling and mechanically lifting?
2.4	What are the procedures for safe lifting?

2.5	Why is it important to use site safety equipment when handling materials and equipment?
2.6	List FOUR aids that may be available to assist manual handling in the workplace. 1 2 3 4
2.7	How do you work safely, follow procedures and report problems when carrying out manual handling?

Section 3 Questions
The importance of working safely at height in the workplace.

3.1	What is 'working at height'?
3.2	What are your responsibilities whilst working at height?
3.3.1	What are the hazards/risks associated with dropping tools and debris from height?
3.3.2	What are the hazards/risks associated with ladders?
3.3.3	What are the hazards/risks associated with overhead cables?
3.3.4	What are the hazards/risks associated with fragile roofs?
3.3.5	What are the hazards/risks associated with tube scaffolds?

3.3.6	What are the hazards/risks associated with mobile scaffolds?
3.3.7	What are the hazards/risks associated with internal voids?
3.3.8	What are the hazards/risks associated with equipment when working at height?
3.3.9	What are the hazards/risks associated with the working area when working at height?
3.3.10	What are the hazards/risks associated with other people when working at height?.
3.4	How can hazards/risks associated with working at height be controlled?
3.5	What is the regulation that controls the use of suitable equipment for working at height?

Section 4 Questions
The risks to health within a construction environment.

4.1	List substances hazardous to health
4.2	List FIVE common risks to health within a construction environment. 1 2 3 4 5
4.3	What the types of hazards/risks are linked with use of drugs and alcohol?
4.4	Why is it important to store combustibles and chemicals correctly?
4.5	Why is personal hygiene important on a construction site?

4.6	What are the dangers of asbestos?
4.7	Give TWO examples of where could you find asbestos waste. 1 2
4.8	What THREE items of personal protective equipment (PPE) should you use when working with hazardous materials. 1 2 3

Section 5 Questions
The importance of working around plant and equipment safely.

5.1	How can moving machinery can cause injuries?
5.2	List FIVE hazards/risks when you use plant and equipment? 1 2 3 4 5
5.3	Why is it important to keep a safe distance away from plant/machinery and equipment until clear contact is made with the operator?
5.4	How can method statements assist in ensuring workers are safe where moving plant is in use?

5.5	How can you eliminate or control hazards/risks relating to working around plant and equipment?
5.6	What do the following signs mean?